EMINEM............

EMINEM BIOGRAPHY FOR KIDS:
THE BOY WHO TURNED HIS WORDS INTO POWER –
THE FASTEST RAPPER WITH THE BIGGEST HEART

Written by
LUIS B. BRISTOL

EMINEM............

Copyright ©2025 All rights reserved by Luis B. Bristol

No part of this publication may be reproduced or transmitted in any form or by any means including photocopying, recording or other electronic or mechanical methods without the prior written permission of the publisher except in the case of brief quotations embodied in critical reviews and certain other non-commercial uses- permitted by copyright

EMINEM............

TABLE OF CONTENTS

Introduction...........................5

Chapter 1: A Boy Named Marshall – The Early Years.......................9

Chapter 2: Battling the Odds – The Road to Rap......................14

Chapter 3: The Slim Shady Era – A Star Is Born......................20

Chapter 4: The Marshall Mathers Story – Success and Struggles......................25

Chapter 5: 8 Mile – The Movie That Changed Everything......................31

Chapter 6: The Comeback – Overcoming Life's Hardest Battles......................38

Chapter 7: Rap God – Breaking Records Again!......................42

EMINEM.............

Chapter 8: Kamikaze and Music to Be Murdered By – Still on Top..46

Chapter 10: Eminem's Fun Side – More Than Just a Rapper..60

Chapter 11: Awards, Achievements, and the Hall of Fame..70

Chapter 12: Eminem's Words of Wisdom – Lessons for Young Dreamers....................................81

Eminem Trivia Challenge – Test Your Knowledge!...............................,............94

Conclusion.......................................103

Answer keys.................................108

EMINEM.............

Introduction

Imagine standing in front of a roaring crowd, microphone in hand, heart pounding. The music drops, and in seconds, your words flow like lightning—fast, sharp, unstoppable. Every syllable, every rhyme, every beat tells a story, a struggle, a victory. This is what Eminem does. But long before he became a rap legend, he was just a boy with a dream, a notebook full of rhymes, and a life that wasn't always kind to him. Marshall Bruce Mathers III, better known as Eminem, wasn't born into fame or fortune. No silver spoon, no easy road—just a kid in a rough neighborhood with a head full of words and a heart full of determination. If you asked the world back then if this skinny, shy boy from Detroit would one day be

EMINEM.............

crowned the Rap God, many would have laughed. But Eminem wasn't the kind to listen to doubters. He didn't just prove them wrong—he shattered every expectation.
His life was like one of his rap battles—full of hard hits, fast comebacks, and moments where it seemed like the fight was over. He faced bullies, poverty, and heartbreak. He got knocked down, but every time, he got back up stronger. He wasn't just rapping for fun; he was fighting to survive, using words as his weapon, turning pain into poetry.

And the world? The world had never seen anything like him.

From freestyle battles in Detroit's underground rap scene to the biggest music stages in the world, Eminem's rise to fame

EMINEM.............

was nothing short of extraordinary. He faced rejection, but he never quit. He was told he'd never make it, but he refused to listen. He went from a kid writing rhymes in a broken notebook to a superstar holding Grammy Awards, setting world records, and inspiring millions with his lyrics.

But fame wasn't the end of the story—it was just the beginning. With success came new battles: critics who doubted him, personal struggles that tested him, and obstacles that could have ended his career. Yet, every time life threw challenges his way, Eminem responded the only way he knew how—with music. His words became louder, his message stronger, his story more powerful.

In this book, you'll discover the real story behind the rapper—the boy who grew up

EMINEM.............

without much but built an empire with his words. You'll learn about his toughest battles, his biggest victories, and the moments that made him a legend. You'll find out what makes Eminem more than just a rapper—what makes him a fighter, a storyteller, and a hero to so many fans around the world.

Are you ready to explore the incredible journey of a boy who turned his words into power? Buckle up, because this is the story of Eminem—the fastest rapper with the biggest heart.

Chapter 1: A Boy Named Marshall – The Early Years

Once upon a time, on October 17, 1972, in a small hospital in St. Joseph, Missouri, a baby boy was born. His mother, Debbie Mathers, looked at her son and named him Marshall Bruce Mathers III. Little did she know, this tiny boy would grow up to change the world of music forever.

Marshall's early years were filled with constant changes. His father, Marshall Mathers Jr., left when he was just a baby, leaving Debbie to raise him on her own. Life was tough, and they didn't have much money. They moved from house to house, trying to find a place to call home.

EMINEM.............

By the time Marshall was a little boy, they had settled in Detroit, Michigan. But even in Detroit, things weren't easy. The neighborhood was rough, and school was even tougher. Marshall struggled to fit in. He was often bullied, and his small size made him an easy target. But there was one thing that set him apart—his love for words.

A Kid with a Big Imagination

Marshall wasn't like the other kids at school. While some loved sports or playing outside, he loved storytelling. He would spend hours making up stories, writing poems, and creating rhymes. But school was a challenge for him. He had trouble keeping up with his classes and was even held back in ninth grade three times. Eventually, he dropped out of high school, but that didn't mean he gave up on learning. Instead, he found his own way to educate himself—through music.

One day, everything changed. Marshall discovered something magical: hip-hop music. It wasn't just regular songs—it was powerful poetry spoken over beats. The rhythm, the energy, the way rappers could tell their life stories through rhymes—it all felt like it was made just for him. He listened to artists like LL Cool J, Run-D.M.C., and the Beastie Boys, amazed at how they turned words into music.

Soon, Marshall started writing his own rhymes. He practiced for hours, trying to

EMINEM.............

make his words flow just like the rappers he admired. He started rapping with his friends, joining local rap battles where he had to prove himself against other talented artists. But there was one problem—he was different. Most rappers were African American, and here he was, a skinny white kid trying to make a name in a world where he didn't seem to belong.

Despite the challenges, Marshall refused to give up. He knew he had something special—his words, his passion, and his determination. Every night, he would practice his raps, making sure his lyrics were faster, sharper, and more creative than anyone else's.

EMINEM.............

But he needed a name, something that would make him stand out. He decided to take the first letters of his name, "M" and "M," and turned it into something unique—Eminem.

No one knew it yet, but Marshall Bruce Mathers III was about to become something extraordinary. The world would soon know his name—not just as a rapper, but as one of the greatest musicians of all time.

Chapter 2: Battling the Odds – The Road to Rap

Marshall was just a kid when he realized that words had power. They could tell stories, express emotions, and even fight back against the tough times in life. But before he became the superstar we now know as Eminem, he had to battle against the odds. And believe me, the road wasn't easy.

It all started when Marshall was around 14 years old. He and his best friend, Proof, would spend hours listening to rap music, memorizing lyrics, and even trying to write their own rhymes. They were inspired by hip-hop legends like LL Cool J, Run-D.M.C., and the Beastie Boys. Rap wasn't just music for Marshall—it was a way to express himself when he felt like no one was listening.

But there was one problem: rap battles in Detroit were dominated by African American artists. A white kid trying to make it in hip-hop? People didn't take him seriously at first. But Marshall wasn't about to give up.

Facing Rejection and Pushing Forward

Marshall started entering local rap battles, stepping up to the mic against some of the best freestyle rappers in the city. At first, people laughed. They thought he didn't belong. But the moment he opened his mouth and let the words flow, the laughter stopped. His rhymes were sharp, his flow was fast, and his punchlines were fierce. He earned respect the hard way—by proving himself battle after battle.

Still, success didn't come easy. He faced rejection after rejection from record labels. Some thought his style was too aggressive. Others just didn't think a white rapper could make it big. He was broke, working minimum-wage jobs to support himself while chasing his dream. He even faced moments of homelessness, sleeping in his car when he had nowhere else to go.

The Birth of Slim Shady

EMINEM.............

During one of his lowest moments, something inside Marshall snapped. He needed a way to channel his anger, frustration, and struggles into something powerful. That's when he created Slim Shady—his rap alter ego. Slim Shady was fearless, loud, and unapologetic. He said things Marshall Mathers was too afraid to say. With this new persona, Marshall poured his heart into his music, writing lyrics that were raw, emotional, and sometimes shocking.

In 1997, he released The Slim Shady EP, an independent project that caught the attention of someone who would change his life forever—Dr. Dre.

EMINEM.............

Meeting Dr. Dre – A Life-Changing Moment

Dr. Dre, one of the most influential producers in hip-hop history, heard Marshall's tape and was blown away. He knew talent when he saw it. Against the advice of many, Dre decided to take a chance on Marshall. When they first met, Marshall was nervous. Here he was, standing in front of a legend, hoping for a shot.

But Dre wasn't just impressed—he was excited. The two started working together immediately, and the result was magic. With Dre's beats and Marshall's explosive lyrics, they created The Slim Shady LP. It was bold,

EMINEM.............

funny, and unlike anything else in hip-hop at the time.

Marshall had finally made it into the big leagues. But this was just the beginning. With a new name, a new sound, and a record deal, the world was about to meet Eminem—the rapper who would change the music industry forever.

Chapter 3: The Slim Shady Era – A Star Is Born

Marshall had been fighting his way up for years, rapping in underground clubs, working odd jobs, and pushing through every setback life threw at him. But in 1997, something happened that would change everything. He created someone new—a wild, fearless, and rebellious character who would take the world by storm. That character was Slim Shady.

By the time Marshall created his Slim Shady persona, he had already been rapping for years. But he was still struggling to get noticed outside of Detroit. Then, one day, his demo tape landed in the hands of one of

EMINEM.............

the biggest producers in hip-hop history—Dr. Dre.

Dr. Dre, who had discovered and produced some of the greatest rappers of all time, was blown away by Marshall's unique flow and raw lyrics. "Find him. Now," he told his team. Soon after, Marshall got the call that changed his life. He was going to meet Dr. Dre.

When they met in the studio, Dre played a beat, and Marshall instantly started rapping. Dre was amazed. It was clear—Marshall wasn't just another rapper. He was a game-changer. That day, they began working on an album that would shake the music world.

EMINEM.............

The Making of The Slim Shady LP

With Dr. Dre as his mentor and producer, Marshall recorded The Slim Shady LP. This album introduced the world to Slim Shady—a mischievous, bold, and darkly humorous alter ego that allowed Marshall to express his frustrations and struggles in a powerful way. The songs were edgy, sometimes funny, sometimes shocking, but always full of skill and creativity.

The album featured hits like My Name Is, which became an instant sensation. The music video, showing Marshall as different wacky characters, was played everywhere. Suddenly, the kid who had once been bullied in school was a superstar. The Slim Shady

LP went triple platinum, and Eminem won his first Grammy for Best Rap Album.

Why Was Eminem's Music Different?

In a world where rap was dominated by artists talking about wealth and success, Marshall's music stood out. He rapped about real struggles—poverty, family problems, self-doubt—but with incredible wordplay and storytelling. He wasn't afraid to be brutally honest, and fans connected with his raw emotions.

But not everyone was a fan. Some people thought his lyrics were too intense or controversial. Marshall knew this, but he believed music should be real, even if it

EMINEM.............

made people uncomfortable. He wanted to tell the truth, no matter what.

His First Grammy Win!

In 2000, the world was watching as Eminem took the stage at the Grammy Awards. Just a few years earlier, he had been struggling to buy food. Now, he was accepting an award for Best Rap Album in front of millions of people. It was a surreal moment—proof that dreams could come true, no matter where you came from.

But Marshall wasn't done yet. This was just the beginning of something even bigger...

24

Chapter 4: The Marshall Mathers Story – Success and Struggles

Marshall had made it. He wasn't just a rapper from Detroit anymore—he was Eminem, a global superstar. But with fame came challenges, and the road ahead wasn't going to be easy.

The Marshall Mathers LP – Breaking Records and Stirring Controversy

In 2000, Eminem released The Marshall Mathers LP, and it became one of the fastest-selling rap albums in history. It sold over 1.7 million copies in its first week! Fans couldn't get enough of his powerful storytelling, razor-sharp lyrics, and fearless attitude. Songs like "Stan," "The Way I Am," and "The Real Slim Shady" took the world by storm.

But while Eminem's fans celebrated his music, critics and parents weren't as thrilled. His lyrics were often raw, emotional, and sometimes controversial. Many accused him of being too aggressive, and some even wanted his albums banned. But Eminem didn't back down—he kept rapping about his real-life struggles, no matter how uncomfortable it made people feel.

Quote: "I say what I want to say and do what I want to do. There's no in-between." – Eminem

EMINEM.............

As Eminem's success skyrocketed, his personal life became more complicated. His relationship with Kim, Hailie's mother, was rocky, and they were constantly in and out of love. The pressure of fame, endless media attention, and personal battles weighed heavily on him.

Despite his struggles, one thing remained constant—his love for his daughter, Hailie. He often mentioned her in his songs, making it clear that she was the most important person in his life. One of his most heartfelt tracks, "Hailie's Song," gave fans a glimpse into his love and dedication to his little girl.

Facing His Own Demons

EMINEM.............

With all the success came overwhelming pressure. Eminem's lyrics weren't just about other people's struggles anymore—they were about his own battles, too. He started relying on prescription drugs to deal with stress and exhaustion, but it wasn't a healthy solution. His friends and family started to worry about him, but Eminem kept pushing forward.

In 2002, he released The Eminem Show, another massive hit. Songs like "Without Me," "Cleanin' Out My Closet," and "Sing for the Moment" cemented his place as one of the greatest rappers of all time. The album sold millions and earned him even more awards, including a Grammy.

But even as he stood on top of the world, Eminem knew something wasn't right. The pressures of fame, personal problems, and growing addiction would soon push him to his breaking point.

Quote: "The truth is, you don't know what is going to happen tomorrow. Life is a crazy ride, and nothing is guaranteed." – Eminem

The Fastest Rap Verse – A Record-Breaking Moment

Even in the middle of his struggles, Eminem kept pushing the limits of rap. He was known for his rapid-fire lyrics, but in 2013, he outdid himself with "Rap God." The song

EMINEM.............

featured one of the fastest rap verses ever recorded—he spit out 97 words in just 15 seconds! This incredible feat earned him a spot in the Guinness World Records.

Eminem's journey was far from over. He had faced battles before, but his biggest challenge was yet to come. Could he overcome his struggles and find his way back to the top? The world was about to find out...

Chapter 5: 8 Mile – The Movie That Changed Everything

Eminem had already made a name for himself in the music world, but in 2002, he did something that no one expected—he became a movie star. And not just any movie star—he played the lead role in a film inspired by his own life. That movie was 8 Mile, and it became a game-changer, not just for Eminem, but for hip-hop in Hollywood.

When Eminem was approached with the idea of making a movie, he wasn't sure if he could do it. He had no experience acting, and stepping into the world of Hollywood felt completely different from battling

EMINEM.............

rappers on the streets of Detroit. But 8 Mile wasn't just any film—it was a story that closely mirrored his own journey.

The movie follows Jimmy "B-Rabbit" Smith Jr., a young aspiring rapper from Detroit who struggles to break into the hip-hop scene while dealing with personal hardships. Sound familiar? That's because much of the story was inspired by Eminem's real life. Just like B-Rabbit, Eminem grew up in a tough neighborhood, faced challenges at home, and had to prove himself in rap battles to earn respect.

Eminem took the role seriously. He didn't just want to play a rapper—he wanted to make the character feel real. To prepare, he trained with acting coaches and spent hours studying how to bring out emotions on screen. He even lost a lot of weight to fit the look of a struggling artist.

Filming was intense. Many scenes were shot in Detroit, including the famous rap battle scenes that took place in an old club. The atmosphere was raw and electric, just like real underground rap battles. Eminem would later admit that the process was exhausting, sometimes filming for 16 hours a day, but he pushed through because he wanted to tell the story right.

When 8 Mile hit theaters in November 2002, it was a massive success. Fans and critics loved it, praising Eminem's performance. Many were surprised by how natural he was on screen, and the movie

EMINEM.............

became a cultural phenomenon. It wasn't just a great film—it was proof that hip-hop stories could be powerful and meaningful in Hollywood.

One of the biggest moments of the film was the final battle scene, where B-Rabbit faces off against his biggest rival in an intense freestyle showdown. The energy, the rhymes, and the emotions in that scene were so powerful that it became one of the most iconic moments in rap history.

"Lose Yourself" – The Song That Made History

Perhaps the biggest achievement from 8 Mile wasn't just the movie—it was the song that came with it. Lose Yourself, the movie's

EMINEM.............

theme song, became one of the most powerful anthems of all time. The lyrics were about seizing the moment, pushing past fear, and giving everything you have to chase your dreams.

"Look, if you had one shot, or one opportunity, to seize everything you ever wanted, in one moment, would you capture it, or just let it slip?"

These opening lines became legendary. The song was everywhere—on the radio, in sports arenas, and on people's playlists when they needed motivation. It became so big that it won an Academy Award (also known as an Oscar) for Best Original Song in 2003. That made Eminem the first rapper in history to win an Oscar! But in true

EMINEM.............

Eminem fashion, he didn't even show up to the award ceremony—he was at home, asleep, thinking he had no chance of winning.

After 8 Mile, Eminem wasn't just a rap star anymore—he was a global icon. The movie introduced his story to millions of new fans who may not have followed hip-hop before. It also proved that rap could be more than just music; it could tell deep, emotional stories that connected with people from all backgrounds.

Even today, 8 Mile remains one of the best hip-hop movies ever made. It showed the world that Eminem's journey wasn't just about music—it was about struggle, perseverance, and never giving up, no

EMINEM..............

matter how many times life tries to knock you down.

With his music and now a successful movie under his belt, what was next for Eminem? The road ahead would be filled with even more challenges—but also one of the greatest comebacks in music history.

Chapter 6: The Comeback – Overcoming Life's Hardest Battles

For a while, it seemed like the world had lost Eminem. The rapper who had once dominated the charts, battled his way through life's toughest challenges, and made millions of fans believe in the power of words had disappeared. His music stopped coming, and his voice grew silent. But what happened to Marshall Mathers? And how did he fight his way back?

By the mid-2000s, Eminem's life had taken a dark turn. His best friend, Proof, had been killed in 2006, a tragedy that left him devastated. At the same time, he was battling personal demons—addiction to

EMINEM.............

prescription pills and depression. The once unstoppable rap star found himself struggling to keep going. He isolated himself from the world, unsure if he would ever make music again.

But deep inside, the fire never died.

The Road to Recovery

Determined to take back control of his life, Eminem knew he had to change. He checked into rehab and fought through the toughest battle of his life—getting clean. It wasn't easy, but he refused to give up. He wanted to be there for his daughter, Hailie, and he wanted to prove to himself that he could rise again.

EMINEM.............

With time, his strength returned, and so did his hunger for music. He started writing again, pouring his struggles into his lyrics. He wasn't just making songs—he was telling his story.

Relapse and Recovery – The Comeback Albums

In 2009, after years of silence, Eminem released Relapse, an album that showed he was back but still struggling with his past. Though it had its hits, some fans felt something was missing. Eminem agreed. He wasn't done. He had more to say.

Just a year later, in 2010, he released Recovery—an album that truly showed his transformation. It wasn't just about rap battles or funny rhymes anymore. It was personal. Songs like Not Afraid and Love the Way You Lie (featuring Rihanna) touched millions. Not Afraid became an anthem of hope, proving that anyone could rise from rock bottom.

Recovery became one of the best-selling albums of the year. Eminem had done the impossible—he had returned stronger than ever. Fans around the world cheered. He wasn't just a rap legend; he was an inspiration. He had fought against the toughest challenges and won.

Eminem's comeback wasn't just about music—it was about proving that no matter how many times life knocks you down, you can always stand up again.

Chapter 7: Rap God – Breaking Records Again!

Eminem had already cemented his legacy as one of the greatest rappers of all time, but he wasn't done yet. Just when people thought he might slow down, he proved everyone wrong. With the release of The Marshall Mathers LP 2 in 2013, he reminded the world why he was called a rap legend. And in this album, one song stood out above the rest—Rap God.

On October 15, 2013, Eminem released Rap God, a song that would go down in history. The track featured a mind-blowing speed rap section, where he rapped 97 words in just 15 seconds! That's over six words per second. It was a feat no one had ever seen before, and it earned him a spot in the Guinness World Records for the most words rapped in a hit single—1,560 words in just six minutes and four seconds.

The song wasn't just about speed. It was a history lesson on hip-hop. Eminem paid tribute to rap legends like Rakim, Tupac Shakur, and N.W.A. He also showed off his lyrical skills, using clever wordplay, references, and rhymes that twisted and turned in ways no one expected. Young fans were left in awe, wondering how a human could even rap that fast!

Collaborating with New Artists

EMINEM.............

Eminem didn't just break records—he also kept up with the younger generation of rappers. He collaborated with artists like Kendrick Lamar on Love Game, and he worked with Rihanna again for The Monster, which became another No. 1 hit. He showed that even after two decades in the industry, he was still at the top of his game.

Another song that made a big impact around this time was Not Afraid. Released in 2010 as part of his Recovery album, this song became an anthem of hope and perseverance. Eminem opened up about his struggles, telling fans that no matter how tough life gets, they should never give up. The song won a Grammy for Best Rap Solo

Performance and was performed in front of thousands of screaming fans worldwide.

By this point, Eminem wasn't just the "angry rapper" anymore—he had evolved. He was now seen as an artist who could inspire, motivate, and still deliver jaw-dropping rhymes. He proved that he wasn't just living off past success. He was still breaking new ground and setting records that would be hard for anyone to beat.

EMINEM............

Chapter 8: Kamikaze and Music to Be Murdered By – Still on Top

Eminem had already made his mark on the world, but even after so many hits, he wasn't ready to rest. Instead, he shocked the world with two surprise albums that proved he was still the king of rap.

On August 31, 2018, Eminem dropped Kamikaze without warning. It was as if he had something to prove. The album was full of fast-paced, hard-hitting tracks that sent a clear message: He wasn't going anywhere. Kamikaze became a hit almost instantly, with songs like Lucky You featuring Joyner Lucas and Fall, which showed that Eminem wasn't afraid to call out his critics.

Responding to Critics

Eminem had faced a lot of criticism over the years, and Kamikaze was his response. Many rappers and fans had said that Eminem had lost his touch, but Kamikaze was his way of showing them he still had the skills. In the song The Ringer, he fired back at his critics, spitting fire with lyrics that no one could deny. Eminem was still the fastest, still the smartest, and still at the top of his game.

Music to Be Murdered By – Another No. 1 Album

In January 2020, Eminem returned once again with Music to Be Murdered By. Like

Kamikaze, this album dropped unexpectedly, surprising fans and critics alike. It became his 10th No. 1 album on the Billboard 200 chart. Tracks like Godzilla and Darkness showed Eminem's ability to mix deep, meaningful lyrics with hard-hitting beats.

The Controversy of Music to Be Murdered By

Despite the album's success, Music to Be Murdered By was not without its controversy. One song, Unaccommodating, included a reference to the 2017 Manchester Arena bombing, which led to public backlash. Though Eminem later apologized for the lyric, the incident showed just how much power his words held. His ability to make headlines with every song proved that he was still one of the most talked-about artists in the world.

Still Unstoppable

Even after all the years, controversies, and ups and downs, Eminem had proven time and again that he was still relevant in the rap game. His willingness to push boundaries, address his critics, and surprise his fans kept him at the top. With his legacy growing even stronger, Eminem continued to show that there was no slowing him down.

His willingness to push boundaries, address his critics, and surprise his fans kept him at the top. With his legacy growing even

EMINEM.............

stronger, Eminem continued to show that there was no slowing him down.

Chapter 9: The Legacy of Eminem – What Makes Him a Legend?

Eminem's career has been nothing short of a rollercoaster ride. From his early struggles to his rise as one of the most famous and influential rap artists in the world, his journey is one of perseverance, talent, and never backing down. But what exactly makes Eminem a legend? Let's break it down.

Eminem didn't just enter the rap game—he changed it. When he first started, there weren't many rappers who looked like him or came from the same background. But that didn't stop him. Instead, Eminem used his unique perspective to bring something

EMINEM.............

new to the table. His witty wordplay, fast rapping, and honest lyrics caught the attention of people all over the world. He rapped about real issues, from growing up in poverty to struggling with fame, addiction, and family troubles. His music resonated with fans from all walks of life because it wasn't just about having fun—it was about telling stories that mattered.

One of the things that set Eminem apart was his ability to tackle tough subjects without sugar-coating them. He wasn't afraid to talk about his personal struggles or address controversial topics, even if it meant upsetting people. In doing so, he made rap music a space where people could be honest about their feelings and experiences. He

EMINEM.............

showed everyone that being real was the key to success in the music industry.

Eminem's influence extends far beyond his own music. Today, you can hear his impact in the music of artists from all genres. His style, characterized by complex rhymes, rapid-fire delivery, and storytelling, has been adopted by countless rappers who grew up listening to him. He paved the way for a new generation of artists who aren't afraid to push boundaries, challenge norms, and speak their truth.

Artists like Kendrick Lamar, J. Cole, Logic, and many others have cited Eminem as an inspiration. His work ethic, authenticity, and raw emotion have shaped the sound of modern rap and hip-hop. Without Eminem,

EMINEM.............

it's possible that some of today's biggest names wouldn't have found the confidence to pursue their dreams in the way they have.

One of the coolest things about Eminem is that he's always evolving. When he first burst onto the scene with The Slim Shady LP in 1999, he had a rebellious, over-the-top style that shocked people. His alter ego, Slim Shady, was wild, unpredictable, and didn't care what anyone thought. But as Eminem grew older and his life changed, so did his music. He started to write more introspective songs, dealing with his struggles with fame, addiction, and relationships.

Albums like The Marshall Mathers LP and The Eminem Show showcased his ability to

EMINEM.............

mix serious topics with rapid-fire rapping and humor. As he got older, his rapping became more complex. His wordplay reached new heights, and his ability to switch between different rap styles—fast, slow, angry, emotional—was unmatched. Eminem didn't just stay the same; he grew with the times, and his music reflected that evolution.

What's even more amazing is that Eminem has stayed relevant for over two decades. In a world where trends change quickly and many artists fade into obscurity, Eminem has managed to maintain his position at the top. His albums continue to top the charts, his music videos rack up millions of views, and his concerts are sold out worldwide.

EMINEM.............

A big part of his staying power is his connection with his fans. Eminem's music speaks to people who feel like they don't fit in or who are going through tough times. His lyrics give them a voice and let them know they're not alone. Eminem's ability to connect with his fans is one of the reasons he's built such a loyal following.

But his music isn't just about being relatable—it's also about pushing boundaries. Eminem isn't afraid to take risks, try new things, and make music that challenges the status quo. He's constantly evolving, experimenting with new sounds, and staying one step ahead of the curve. This willingness to grow and change is one of the reasons why he's such a legend in the music world.

EMINEM............

At the heart of Eminem's success is his ability with words. He's often called one of the greatest lyricists of all time, and for good reason. Eminem has a unique gift for crafting intricate rhymes and spitting them out at lightning speed. But what really sets him apart is his ability to tell a story through his lyrics.

Whether he's rapping about his personal struggles, making fun of the world around him, or speaking up for the underdog, Eminem's words always pack a punch. His music has inspired millions of people and helped them get through difficult times. That's the true power of Eminem's legacy: His words are more than just songs—they're a reflection of his life, his struggles, and his triumphs. And through it all, he's shown that anything is possible if you keep fighting for it.

So, what makes Eminem stand out from all the other rap legends? It's a combination of his talent, work ethic, and authenticity. Eminem has faced more challenges than most people could imagine, yet he's always come out on top. He's been knocked down by critics, by addiction, by personal loss, but he's never stayed down for long. Instead, he's used every setback as fuel for his next big success.

In a genre known for boasting and bravado, Eminem has always remained true to himself. He's never been afraid to show his vulnerabilities, his insecurities, and his flaws. And because of that, he's become one of the most relatable artists in the world. His

EMINEM.............

fans don't just love his music—they admire his strength, his resilience, and his willingness to face the truth, no matter how difficult it may be.

Quote: "Success is my only option, failure's not." – Eminem

Chapter 10: Eminem's Fun Side – More Than Just a Rapper

While Eminem is known for his intense, hard-hitting rap lyrics and his powerful impact on the music industry, there's another side to him that many people might not realize: his fun, quirky, and playful personality. When he's not rapping, Eminem has a great sense of humor and loves to enjoy life in ways that make people laugh and appreciate him even more. Let's take a closer look at some of the lighter moments of Eminem's life.

Funny Interviews and Jokes

EMINEM.............

Eminem might be serious when it comes to his music, but when it comes to interviews, he's known for his quick wit and sense of humor. He's often seen making funny jokes, teasing reporters, or even getting into silly situations that make everyone laugh. His sharp tongue and sarcastic humor have become a huge part of his persona. In fact, many fans look forward to seeing what funny thing Eminem will say next during his interviews!

One memorable moment came during an interview on The Ellen DeGeneres Show. When Ellen asked Eminem if he would ever be interested in acting in a movie, he jokingly responded, "If they made a movie about me, it would probably be a cartoon." He laughed and added that he'd probably be the type to play an exaggerated, funny version of himself, which definitely showed his more playful side.

Eminem's humor isn't just about making jokes—it's also about not taking himself too seriously. He loves to poke fun at his own image and the way people see him. Whether it's joking about his alter ego, Slim Shady, or making fun of his fame, Eminem doesn't mind laughing at the crazy situations he's been in. This ability to laugh at himself has helped him connect with his fans in a different way.

Eminem and His Love for Cartoons

Believe it or not, Eminem has a big love for cartoons! Many of his fans know about his

EMINEM............

admiration for the Looney Tunes, and it's no surprise that some of the animated characters and stories from his childhood had an influence on his music. Growing up, Eminem was a fan of cartoons like Tom and Jerry, The Simpsons, and Family Guy—all of which are known for their wild humor and unpredictable characters.

In fact, The Simpsons made a guest appearance with Eminem in an episode where he voiced himself. The episode, called "The Real Slim Shady," featured Eminem poking fun at his own persona and making light of his image as a controversial rapper. This was just another example of how Eminem isn't afraid to embrace his fun side and show his fans that, behind the intense

EMINEM.............

rapper, there's a guy who loves to kick back and enjoy some classic TV shows.

But Eminem's love for cartoons goes beyond just watching them. He's used animation in his own music videos, like the one for his hit song "Without Me." In the video, Eminem is transformed into an animated character who bounces around in a cartoon world, all while delivering his iconic rap verses. This creative choice showed how Eminem enjoys mixing fun and imagination with his art. He's not just about the music—he's also about entertaining his fans in unique and interesting ways.

Eminem and His Hobbies Outside of Music

EMINEM............

When Eminem isn't working on music, he enjoys doing some pretty fun things that help him relax and recharge. One of his favorite pastimes is playing video games. Over the years, Eminem has mentioned in interviews how much he loves gaming, and he's even shared some of his favorite games with fans. From sports games to first-person shooters, Eminem has been known to get totally immersed in the virtual world.

He also loves spending time with his family. Although Eminem's life is often filled with the demands of being a superstar, he values his privacy and cherishes moments with his loved ones. Whether it's hanging out with his daughter, Hailie, or enjoying time with his close friends, Eminem makes sure to balance his professional life with his personal one. This shows that, despite being one of the biggest names in music, he's still just a regular person who enjoys the simple things in life.

In addition to gaming and family time, Eminem has also been known to enjoy a good laugh over movies. His sense of humor can often be seen in his love for comedy films, and he has even made references to his favorite comedy moments in his music. Like any regular person, Eminem enjoys unwinding with a good movie that makes him laugh, and that fun side definitely comes out in his music and interviews.

Fun Fact: Eminem's World Record for Rapping

EMINEM.............

Did you know that Eminem once set a world record for rapping? In 2013, he broke the Guinness World Record for the most words in a hit single when he rapped an incredible 1,560 words in his song "Rap God." The song is a display of Eminem's lightning-fast rapping skills, and it became a huge hit among fans. The world record was just another way that Eminem showed off his crazy talent—but it also shows just how much he loves to push himself and break new barriers, all while having fun with his craft.

Eminem's Love for Social Media and Memes

Eminem is also pretty active on social media, where he shares his thoughts,

EMINEM.............

interacts with fans, and, of course, enjoys a bit of humor. Known for his playful interactions on platforms like Twitter, Eminem has a knack for trolling and making memes that reflect his sarcastic, witty personality. He enjoys keeping his fans entertained, whether it's with a funny post or responding to jokes and memes that his fans create about him.

His sense of humor extends to his social media presence as well. One of his funniest moments on Twitter came when he took to the platform to post a meme of himself holding a bottle of ketchup, along with the caption, "Ketchup on everything." It was just a random, fun post that had fans laughing and showing how even Eminem can enjoy a good joke.

EMINEM............

A Rapper Who Loves to Have Fun

Eminem might be known for his intense, thought-provoking music, but he's also a person who knows how to have fun. Whether he's cracking jokes in interviews, making animated appearances, playing video games, or simply hanging out with his family, Eminem's playful side adds another layer to his already fascinating personality. It's a reminder that even the biggest stars need time to relax and enjoy life—and that sometimes, laughter is just as important as the music.

Chapter 11: Awards, Achievements, and the Hall of Fame

Eminem's journey in the music world is like a roller coaster ride full of ups and downs, but through it all, he has built a legacy that is second to none. From early struggles to becoming a global superstar, Eminem's hard work, determination, and raw talent have earned him countless awards, recognition, and a permanent spot in music history. In this chapter, we're going to dive into some of his most notable achievements and the honors he's received for his groundbreaking career.

Grammy Awards: The Symbol of Music Excellence

EMINEM............

The Grammy Awards are one of the most prestigious honors in the music industry, and Eminem has won many of them over the years. His first Grammy win came in 2000, when his debut album The Slim Shady LP won Best Rap Album. That was just the beginning. Over the years, Eminem's music continued to earn Grammy nominations, and he was able to collect even more trophies, solidifying his place as one of the best in the game.

One of the most memorable moments of his Grammy career was when Eminem won the Best Rap Album award for The Marshall Mathers LP in 2001. That album was a huge turning point in his career, and it showed the world that he wasn't just a one-hit-wonder—he was here to stay. The win was a testament to his storytelling, lyricism, and ability to connect with fans on a personal level.

Eminem's Grammy achievements didn't stop there. He went on to win several more Grammys, including awards for Best Rap Song and Best Rap Performance. His powerful performances at the Grammy Awards, where he would often perform his most iconic songs, helped him build even more excitement around his music. Each Grammy win added to his reputation as one of the greatest and most influential rap artists of all time.

MTV Awards: Dominating the Pop Culture Scene

EMINEM..............

MTV, the channel that has shaped pop culture for decades, has been another major platform for Eminem to showcase his music and win recognition. From the very beginning of his career, Eminem's music videos and performances on MTV captured the attention of millions. His bold and unapologetic style set him apart from other artists, and he quickly became a favorite of both fans and critics alike.

Throughout his career, Eminem has won multiple MTV Video Music Awards (VMAs) for his music videos. His iconic music video for "The Real Slim Shady" earned him a VMA for Best Male Video, and he also won Best Hip-Hop Video for "Lose Yourself." These wins helped to further cement his

EMINEM.............

reputation as a trailblazer in the music industry.

But it wasn't just the music videos that made Eminem a VMA favorite—his live performances were also unforgettable. One of the most talked-about moments in VMA history came when Eminem performed his song "The Monster" with Rihanna at the 2014 MTV Video Music Awards. The performance was electrifying and showcased Eminem's undeniable stage presence. His performances have always been a mix of energy, emotion, and connection with the audience, making each one a memorable event.

An Oscar for "Lose Yourself" – A Hollywood Achievement

EMINEM............

In 2003, Eminem reached an achievement that many never expected: he won an Academy Award (Oscar) for Best Original Song for his hit single "Lose Yourself." This was an incredible moment in his career because it was a rare honor for a rap artist to win an Oscar. The song was featured in the movie 8 Mile, and it became an anthem for anyone who was determined to overcome obstacles and achieve their dreams.

"Lose Yourself" wasn't just any song—it was the soundtrack to the movie that marked Eminem's acting debut. The song's powerful lyrics, which encourage listeners to seize the moment and not let opportunities slip away, became a message of hope and inspiration for many fans. Winning an Oscar for this song was a huge milestone for Eminem, proving that his influence wasn't just limited to music—it was reaching people across all forms of entertainment.

Induction into the Rock & Roll Hall of Fame

In 2022, Eminem was inducted into the Rock & Roll Hall of Fame, solidifying his place in music history alongside other legendary artists like Elvis Presley, The Beatles, and Michael Jackson. The Hall of Fame honors musicians who have made a significant impact on the music industry, and Eminem's induction was a testament to his influence and contributions to the world of music, especially hip-hop.

EMINEM.............

Becoming a member of the Rock & Roll Hall of Fame is a huge honor for any artist, and Eminem's induction marked the culmination of a career that has shaped the music world for over two decades. It was a moment of reflection for Eminem, who had come a long way from his early days in Detroit, battling for respect in rap battles. His induction into the Hall of Fame was not just a recognition of his musical achievements but also a recognition of his impact on pop culture and the way he pushed the boundaries of what rap music could be.

Breaking Records – Eminem's Impact on the Music World

EMINEM.............

Beyond the awards, Eminem has also broken countless records throughout his career, setting new standards in the music industry. He holds several Guinness World Records, including the record for most words in a hit song, thanks to his track "Rap God," in which he raps 1,560 words in just over six minutes. This record-breaking achievement showcased Eminem's insane lyrical ability and his dedication to pushing the limits of what rap music could be.

Eminem has also achieved multiple platinum certifications for his albums, with several of them selling millions of copies worldwide. The Marshall Mathers LP, The Eminem Show, and Recovery are just a few of the albums that have been certified diamond, which means they sold over 10

EMINEM.............

million copies. His influence on the rap genre is immeasurable, and he has helped shape the sound and culture of hip-hop for years to come.

Trivia Challenge: Can You Name Three of Eminem's Biggest Awards?

1. Grammy Awards for Best Rap Album

2. MTV Video Music Awards for Best Hip-Hop Video

3. Oscar for Best Original Song for "Lose Yourself"

EMINEM.............

Eminem's achievements and awards are a testament to his talent, determination, and passion for his craft. He's been recognized for his skills as a rapper, his creativity as a songwriter, and his ability to connect with fans on a deep level. But more than just the awards and accolades, what truly makes Eminem legendary is his ability to inspire millions of people around the world to believe in themselves, overcome challenges, and never give up on their dreams.

Chapter 12: Eminem's Words of Wisdom – Lessons for Young Dreamers

Eminem's story is more than just about rap music, fame, and awards. It's a story of overcoming challenges, facing fears, and believing in yourself, no matter what. As he rose from being a struggling young boy in Detroit to becoming one of the biggest names in music history, Eminem learned a lot along the way. And the lessons he's picked up are ones that can inspire anyone—especially young dreamers like you!

In this chapter, we're going to dive into some of Eminem's most powerful messages.

EMINEM............

These are the lessons he's learned from his struggles and triumphs, the advice he gives to those who want to follow their own dreams, and the wisdom he shares to help others keep going when the road gets tough.

The Power of Perseverance – Never Giving Up

One of the biggest lessons Eminem teaches through his life and music is the importance of perseverance. He didn't become a rap legend overnight. In fact, there were many times when it seemed like his dreams were impossible. He faced rejection after rejection, struggled with personal issues, and dealt with the pressures of fame. But despite all of this, he never gave up.

EMINEM.............

When Eminem was starting out, he faced a lot of criticism. People told him he wouldn't make it because he was from a rough part of town, because he was white in a predominantly Black genre, and because his style was different. But instead of listening to the doubters, Eminem pushed forward. He kept practicing, kept writing, and kept rapping. And eventually, all his hard work paid off.

Eminem's perseverance is a key reason why he became so successful. His motto? "Success is my only option, failure's not." These words remind us that while failure is part of the journey, it doesn't have to define us. If you want something badly enough, you have to keep trying, even when things get hard.

EMINEM............

Overcoming Fear – Embrace Your Own Voice

When Eminem first started rapping, he was terrified. He didn't know if people would like his style, if they would understand his lyrics, or if he would ever make a name for himself. But he faced his fears head-on. He learned to embrace his unique voice, even if it wasn't the popular choice.

In his early days, Eminem spent hours practicing his craft, sometimes in front of a mirror, working on his speed, his flow, and his delivery. He started rapping at local clubs and in freestyle battles, where he would compete against other artists. Though he was nervous, he knew that this was the best way to grow and improve. Over time, he built up the confidence to trust in his abilities.

Eminem's story teaches us that it's okay to be afraid. Fear is something everyone feels, even the most successful people. But what matters is not letting fear stop you from doing what you love. Whether you're an artist, an athlete, or just chasing a big goal, the only way to get better is to keep trying, even when you feel scared.

The Importance of Staying True to Yourself

One thing that sets Eminem apart from many artists is his commitment to being himself. He's never tried to fit into the mold of what people think a rapper should be.

EMINEM.............

Instead, he's always stayed true to his own experiences, emotions, and thoughts, even if they were controversial or misunderstood.

In many of his songs, Eminem shares his struggles with addiction, family issues, and growing up in poverty. He's also used his music to address issues like bullying and feeling like an outsider. His willingness to be vulnerable and honest with his audience has made him a role model for many young people.

Eminem's message here is simple: don't try to be someone you're not. Don't let others pressure you into changing who you are or what you believe. Being yourself is what makes you unique and powerful. When you stay true to yourself, people will respect you for it.

The Value of Hard Work – Practice Makes Perfect

Eminem didn't become the fastest rapper in the world by taking shortcuts. He put in countless hours of practice, writing and rapping every day. He was dedicated to his craft, and he worked hard to make sure he was always improving. Even when he reached the top, he didn't stop practicing. He understood that no matter how successful he became, there was always room for growth.

Eminem's dedication to hard work is something that young dreamers can take to heart. Whether you're trying to be a rapper, an athlete, an artist, or anything else, it's important to put in the effort. Talent can take you far, but hard work is what will get you to the finish line. There's no substitute for putting in the time and effort to improve your skills.

In an interview, Eminem once said, "I'm not afraid to be a work in progress. You can always get better." This mindset is something that anyone who is serious about their dreams should adopt. Never stop learning, never stop growing, and never stop working toward being the best version of yourself.

Turning Struggles into Strengths

EMINEM.............

Eminem has faced many struggles throughout his life, but he's always found a way to turn those struggles into strengths. He grew up in a tough neighborhood, dealt with the loss of loved ones, and battled addiction. But instead of letting these things break him, he channeled his pain into his music.

Through his lyrics, Eminem has been able to connect with people who are going through similar challenges. He uses his story to inspire others and to show them that it's possible to overcome hardships. His ability to turn negative experiences into positive lessons is one of the reasons why his music resonates with so many people.

For young fans, Eminem's story is a reminder that no matter what challenges you face, you have the power to overcome them. Life will throw obstacles in your way, but how you respond to those obstacles is what matters most. Turn your struggles into motivation, and let them drive you forward.

Final Words of Wisdom: "Be Proud of Who You Are"

Eminem has never been afraid to speak his mind or stand up for what he believes in. Whether through his music, interviews, or public appearances, he's always stayed true to himself. His message for young fans is simple: be proud of who you are. No matter where you come from, what you've been through, or what others think of you, always remember that you have the power to achieve great things.

As he once said, "Be proud of who you are. And what you stand for. If people can't accept that, they're not meant to be in your life." This message is one that anyone—young or old—can relate to. You don't need to change who you are to fit in. Your unique qualities and experiences are what make you special.

Lesson Recap: What Can Young Dreamers Learn from Eminem's Journey?

Never Give Up: Perseverance is key to achieving your dreams, no matter how tough things get.

EMINEM.............

Face Your Fears: It's okay to be scared, but don't let fear stop you from pursuing what you love.

Stay True to Yourself: Be yourself, no matter what others think.

Hard Work Pays Off: Practice and dedication are the keys to success.

Turn Struggles into Strengths: Use your challenges as fuel to grow and improve.

Be Proud of Who You Are: Embrace your uniqueness and be confident in who you are.

Eminem's journey shows us that anything is possible when you believe in yourself, work hard, and never give up on your dreams. His

EMINEM..............

story isn't just about rap—it's about resilience, strength, and the power of using your voice to make an impact.

EMINEM............

Eminem Trivia Challenge – Test Your Knowledge!

Are you ready to test how much you know about Eminem? This fun trivia challenge will put your knowledge to the test! Each question has four possible answers—only one is correct. Choose wisely, and see if you can score a perfect 20 out of 20!

1. What is Eminem's real name?
a) Marshall Bruce Mathers III
b) Michael Brandon Mathers
c) Matthew Brian Mathers
d) Mark Benjamin Mathers

2. Where was Eminem born?
a) New York, New York

EMINEM.............

b) Detroit, Michigan

c) Chicago, Illinois

d) Los Angeles, California

3. What was the title of Eminem's first major studio album?

a) The Slim Shady LP

b) Infinite

c) The Eminem Show

d) Encore

4. What year did Eminem release The Marshall Mathers LP?

a) 1997

b) 1998

c) 1999

d) 2000

EMINEM.............

5. Which famous rapper helped Eminem rise to fame?

a) Jay-Z

b) Dr. Dre

c) Snoop Dogg

d) Kanye West

6. What is the name of Eminem's daughter, whom he often raps about?

a) Haley

b) Hailie

c) Hailey

d) Hallie

7. What was Eminem's rap group called before he became a solo artist?

a) D12

b) The Rap Avengers

c) Detroit Kings

EMINEM..............

d) The Underground Crew

8. Which of these songs won Eminem an Academy Award for Best Original Song?
a) Lose Yourself
b) Stan
c) Mockingbird
d) Without Me

9. What is the name of the movie Eminem starred in, based on his own life?
a) Detroit Dreams
b) Rap Star
c) 8 Mile
d) Shady Streets

10. Which album features the hit song Without Me?
a) The Slim Shady LP

EMINEM.............

b) The Eminem Show

c) Encore

d) Relapse

11. What is Eminem's alter ego name in his music?

a) Slim Jimmy

b) Slim Shady

c) Slim Reaper

d) Slim Marshall

12. In which song does Eminem rap the fastest?

a) Rap God

b) Lose Yourself

c) The Way I Am

d) Godzilla

EMINEM............

13. Eminem took a break from music in the mid-2000s. Why?
a) He went on a world tour
b) He started a new business
c) He struggled with addiction and personal issues
d) He retired from music

14. What is the name of Eminem's record label?
a) Aftermath Records
b) Rap God Records
c) Shady Records
d) Slim Shady Music

15. Which famous female singer was featured in Eminem's song Love the Way You Lie?
a) Beyoncé

EMINEM.............

b) Rihanna

c) Alicia Keys

d) Lady Gaga

16. What does the "LP" stand for in The Marshall Mathers LP?

a) Long Play

b) Lyrical Power

c) Legendary Performance

d) Loud Production

17. Which famous comedian and actor appeared in the music video for Just Lose It?

a) Jim Carrey

b) Adam Sandler

c) Will Ferrell

d) Robin Williams

EMINEM............

18. What is the title of Eminem's 2020 album?
a) Revival
b) Music to Be Murdered By
c) Kamikaze
d) Recovery

19. Which song did Eminem perform at the Oscars in 2020?
a) Stan
b) Not Afraid
c) Lose Yourself
d) My Name Is

20. Eminem is often referred to as the "Rap God." Which song solidified this nickname?
a) Stan
b) Rap God
c) The Real Slim Shady

EMINEM.............

d) Mockingbird

Great job on the trivia challenge! Want to know if you got them all right? Check the answers at the end of the book!

Conclusion

As we reach the final chapter of Eminem's incredible journey, one thing is clear—his story is more than just about rap. It's about determination, passion, and the power of words. From a little boy named Marshall Mathers, who struggled to find his place in the world, to the global superstar known as Eminem, his life is proof that dreams can come true if you work hard enough.

Eminem didn't have an easy childhood. He moved from city to city, faced bullying, and struggled in school. But through all of it, he found something that made him feel powerful—music. When the world told him he wouldn't succeed, he turned to rap to express himself. Instead of giving up, he

EMINEM.............

practiced harder, wrote better, and battled his way to the top.

Eminem's lyrics are more than just words—they tell his life story. He raps about struggles, pain, love, and victory. His music has inspired millions of people to believe in themselves, no matter where they come from. He showed young fans that words can be a superpower, and if you use them wisely, they can change the world.

Eminem didn't just become a great rapper—he became one of the greatest. He won Grammy Awards, broke world records, and even won an Oscar. He performed on the biggest stages, collaborated with the biggest artists, and set new standards for rap music. No matter how high he climbed, he never stopped challenging himself to be better.

EMINEM.............

Beyond music, Eminem has shown that he is more than just a rapper. He is a father, a mentor, and someone who gives back to the world. Through his music and his actions, he has taught young fans important lessons—work hard, stay true to yourself, and never let anyone tell you that you're not good enough.
Eminem's story is an inspiration to kids and young fans everywhere. Here are some of the most important lessons from his journey:

Never give up. Even when life gets tough, keep pushing forward.

Believe in yourself. Even if others doubt you, stay confident in your dreams.

EMINEM.............

Work hard. Talent is important, but dedication and practice are what make you great.

Use your voice. Your words have power—use them to tell your story and inspire others. Eminem's journey isn't over. Even after decades in the music industry, he still surprises the world with new music, new records, and new achievements. But no matter what he does next, one thing will never change—he will always be the boy who turned his words into power, the fastest rapper with the biggest heart.
Eminem's story proves that anything is possible. No matter where you start, no matter how hard life gets, you can rise above it. His music will continue to inspire

EMINEM.............

generations of young fans who dream big, work hard, and refuse to give up.
So, the next time you listen to an Eminem song, remember the journey behind the words. And maybe, just maybe, it will inspire you to chase your own dreams—just like he did.

Thank you for joining this journey through the life of Eminem! Keep believing, keep dreaming, and keep writing your own story.

EMINEM.............

Answer keys

Here are the answers to the Eminem Trivia Challenge:

1. a) Marshall Bruce Mathers III
2. b) Detroit, Michigan
3. b) Infinite
4. d) 2000
5. b) Dr. Dre
6. b) Hailie
7. a) D12
8. a) Lose Yourself
9. c) 8 Mile
10. b) The Eminem Show
11. b) Slim Shady
12. d) Godzilla
13. c) He struggled with addiction and personal issues

EMINEM.............

14. c) Shady Records
15. b) Rihanna
16. a) Long Play
17. a) Jim Carrey
18. b) Music to Be Murdered By
19. c) Lose Yourself
20. b) Rap God

Made in the USA
Monee, IL
31 May 2025